REITs

How to Build Passive
Income from Real Estate
Investment Trust

Table of Contents

Preface v

Introduction 1

Chapter 1: What Are REITs? 5

What Are REITs? 5

How Do They Work? 7

Factors That Make a REIT 8

Types of REITs 9

Types of REITs Based on Investment
Holdings 10

Types of REITs Based on Trading Status 11

Common Misconceptions 13

Chapter 2: Should You Invest in REITs? 17

REITs in Today's Markets 17

Other Considerations 19

Why You Should Invest in REITs 20

The Risks of Investing in REITs 24

Risks of Investing in Non-Traded REITs 25

Risks of Investing in Publicly Traded REITs.... 26

Chapter 3: Choosing REIT 29

How to Choose the Right REITs........................ 29
How to Assess a REIT 34
How to Value REIT 37

Chapter 4: Diversifying with REITs 40

What Is Diversification and Why
Is It Important? 40
How to Diversify Your Investment Portfolio 42
Using REITs to Diversify Your Portfolio 45
REIT Sectors That Can Contribute to a
Diversified Portfolio 46

Chapter 5: Getting Started with REITs 51

Step-by-Step Guide: Investing in REITs 51
Common Mistakes to Avoid 55

Conclusion...60

References 63

Preface

Close your eyes and imagine yourself in 10 years. What do you see yourself doing? Chances are, you don't see yourself stuck in an office, working a 9-5 job, and leading a routine life. It's never too early to start saving for retirement or working towards your financial goals and achieving financial freedom. That is why you should consider investing in financial or real estate markets.

This book is a guide to investing in real estate investment trusts and contains easy-to-grasp knowledge and step-by-step methods you can apply in real estate markets.

Best wishes on achieving your financial goals!

Introduction

Actively and consistently saving a portion of your income is an important habit to learn. However, it's not nearly enough to create the future you desire for yourself. If you already have a good sum of money saved up, you should consider investing it in the financial and real estate markets.

Investing your money is one of the easiest and most popular ways to generate passive income, which is the key to building one's wealth. If you learn how to build a diverse investment portfolio, you can increase the value of your money by outpacing inflation. Smart investors compound their investments or reinvest the money they earn through dividends and other earnings to generate more income.

Each type of investment comes with a unique level of potential market risks and returns. While riskier investments offer higher potential returns, you should always offset their risks by investing in safer ventures. REITs are ideal portfolio-building instruments that can be used to neutralize the risk that comes with investing in the stock market. Even though they're less risky than stocks, they offer higher returns than bonds, making them the perfect addition to your investment portfolio.

The sooner you start investing, the faster you can work towards your financial goals and achieve financial freedom. By reading this book, you'll learn everything you need to know about building passive income from real estate investment trusts. You'll learn what REITs are and how they work. You'll also understand the different types of REITs available for trading and how you can get started with each one.

Determining whether a certain investment suits your current needs and goals can be challenging. Fortunately, this ultimate guide explores REITs in today's markets and delves deep into the advantages, disadvantages, and risks of investing in REITs, allowing you to determine if it's right for you. Then, you'll find out how to choose the right REITs to invest in and how to value and assess them.

This book also covers key investment concepts like portfolio diversification. You'll understand what it is, why it's important, and how to do it. You'll learn how to use REITs to diversify your investment portfolio and find out what diversified REITs are good for. Finally, the last chapter serves as a step-by-step guide on how to get started. In it, you'll learn how to start investing, know the common mistakes that beginners make and how to avoid them, and find indispensable tips that will aid you throughout your REIT investment journey.

Chapter 1:

What Are REITs?

I n this chapter, you'll find out what real estate investment trusts are and how they work. You'll understand how they generate income and what qualifies as a REIT. This chapter also explores the different types of REITs by investment holdings and trading status and covers some of the most common misconceptions that people have about them.

What Are REITs?

Investors who aim to build fixed-income or equity portfolios often consider making room for REITs or Real Estate Investment Trusts. This type of investment can be a great way to diversify your portfolio (more on that later!) and increase your returns while lowering your overall risk.

The underlying real estate assets of REITs appreciate in value, which means that your capital does too. This, along with the income you can generate from earning dividends, make REITs a great way to neutralize the risk of investing in other assets like stocks and bonds.

A REIT is any company that finances, owns, manages, or operates real estate properties that generate income. This type of investment follows the same blueprint as mutual funds, which means that the investments of several individuals are pooled in REITs. Each investor can then earn dividends without personally overseeing, buying, or managing the properties or their mortgages.

Many people think that they need to have a very large sum of capital that they're willing to risk for an opportunity to invest in real estate. However, REITs make it possible for anyone who would like to invest in valuable properties, not just hedge funds, wealthy individuals, or banks, to benefit from them through returns and dividend income.

Investing in real estate asset portfolios with REITs is quite similar to investing in other industries. You can do it via ETFs, mutual funds, or even through buying individual company stocks. There are numerous types of REITs that you can explore. Real estate investment trusts are more popular than you think- around 150 million people in the USA alone live in REITs invested properties through several investment funds like pension plans, 401(k)s, and IRAs.

How Do They Work?

REITs were first introduced by congress during the 1960s. This type of investment was initially meant to amend the Cigar Excise Tax Extension. Before this provision was made, the ability to buy real estate portfolio shares in commercial properties could only be completed through financial institutions that served as intermediaries.

REIT portfolios are not limited to certain types of properties. They can comprise infrastructures like energy pipelines and cell towers, warehouses, apartment complexes, houses, healthcare institutions, data centers, office buildings, hotels, self-storage areas, retail centers, and more. While these investments are centered around a certain real estate industry, your portfolio can carry numerous types of properties if you invest in specialty or diversified REITs. You can publicly trade in real estate investment trusts on renowned securities exchanges and buy and sell them as you would with stocks. REITs are highly liquid assets that are usually traded under large volumes.

REITs are currently thought to own over $4.5 trillion in total assets across the United States. Public REITs own around $3 trillion of this amount, and the REITs listed by the United States have over $1.4 trillion of equity market capitalization.

Most REITs follow a similar, easy-to-grasp business model. The company leases property and collects its rent to generate income. This profit is then used to pay dividends to the investors. At least 90% of the taxable income of the real estate property must be paid out to the shareholders, who then pay income taxes on the dividends they receive.

Factors That Make a REIT

Not all real estate companies can qualify as REITs. To meet the qualifications, a company must meet certain IRC provisions. Most notably, these requirements state that the company must be the primary long-term owner of a piece of income-generating real estate. The company must also annually distribute 90% of the generated taxable income to the property's shareholders in the form of dividends.

To qualify as a REIT, 75% of the company's total assets must be invested in U.S. treasuries, cash, or real estate. It should also generate 75% of its total income from the sales of real estate, rents, or interest received on the mortgages used to fund real estate property. REITs should be managed by trustees or a board of directors and gather a minimum of 100 investors after their first year of establishment. The entity should be a taxable corporation and have a maximum of 50% of its shares carried by less than 6 shareholders.

If the company complies with these rules, it won't have to pay corporate taxes, allowing them to fund real estate in a more affordable way. This would also leave them with more profit to distribute among the shareholders in comparison to non-REIT entities. Even if they start small, REITs can eventually pay larger dividends to investors.

Types of REITs

There are three main umbrellas of real estate investment trusts that you can invest in, depending on their investment holdings. These are mortgage, hybrid, and equity REITs. Each of these investment trusts can then be broken down into more types that depend on their trading status: public non-traded, private, and publicly traded REITs. Each investment trust comes with a unique set of characteristics, rewards, and risks. Understanding what each REIT entails will allow you to choose which ones to buy, depending on your needs, capabilities, and investment goals.

Types of REITs Based on Investment Holdings

- **Mortgage REITs**

These companies don't own the underlying real estate. However, they own the debt securities that the real estate property supports. Let's say someone gets a mortgage on a house. A REIT would likely buy this mortgage from its lender so it can collect the monthly payments instead. While the company would be profiting from the interest income, the owner of the house would be responsible for operating and maintaining the property. This type of investment is more profitable than equity REITs because it pays higher dividends, but it's a lot riskier to invest in.

- **Equity REITs**

These companies are responsible for managing the property and all tasks that come with the responsibility of owning real estate- much like landlords. Equity REITs own the real estate at hand, collect their rent checks from the tenants, and are responsible for maintaining and reinvesting money into servicing and operating the property.

- **Hybrid REITs**

Hybrid REITs offer the best of both worlds. They invest in both mortgages and equity, which creates a more balanced investment because they might profit when interest rates rise and fall. Hybrid REITs take on several types of business activities and real estate properties. While they're the least risky option, hybrid REITs are not as common as the other types.

Types of REITs Based on Trading Status

- **Publicly Traded REITs**

These REITs are publicly available on exchanges and can be traded like ETFs and stocks. You can also purchase them through regular brokerage accounts. Currently, over 200 publicly traded REITs are available for trading on the market. These companies are generally more transparent and comply with better governance standards in comparison to private and public non-traded REITs. You'd also be able to buy and sell the underlying stocks a lot faster than other alternatives due to their high liquidity. Many investors, even highly seasoned ones, choose to only engage with publicly traded REITs.

- **Private REITs**

These companies are not listed on exchanges, making them difficult to trade and value. They aren't registered with the SEC either, which is why they have to meet a few disclosure standards and requirements. If you invest in private REITs, you will find it challenging to assess the performance of the company and the investment trust. This makes private REITs the riskiest and least attractive option for investors.

- **Public Non-Traded REITs**

These investment trusts are registered with the SEC, but you can't trade them via an exchange.

They are available at brokers that offer this type of REIT. Since these REITs aren't publicly traded on exchanges, they are highly illiquid, usually for over 8 years. They're also difficult to value - the SEC suggests that it might take up to 18 months after the closing of the offering for public non-traded REITs to estimate the value of the investments.

To start trading either private or public non-traded REITs, you might be requested to pay a higher account minimum. These usually start at $25,000. Their trading fees are also more expensive than publicly traded REITs and are often only available for SEC-classified accredited investors. People who can trade these REITs might need to meet a net worth or annual income minimum.

Common Misconceptions

People often shy away from REITs for all the wrong reasons, which is why we are here to clear up some common misconceptions.

They're Not Ideal for Younger Investors

Has anyone ever told you that REITs aren't the right investment for you unless you're a retiree? REITs have

been long misportrayed as income investments, caus-
ing younger investors to steer toward growth stocks
instead. If you look at the charts, you'll find that, as
opposed to popular belief, REITs do enjoy substantial
growth and offer many rewards beyond the dividends
they offer. On a 20-year average for the period between 1999 and 2019, growth investments have generated around half the annual total returns that RE-
ITs have generated during that time. In other words,
while the S&P 500 generated an average of 7.5% each
year, REITs generated 14%. REITs offer consistent and
resilient growth, making them a great choice for those
interested in both income and growth investments.

They Are Overpriced

If you check the share price for companies with
large market capitalizations, you'll naturally as-
sume that REITs are very overpriced. They're just
like all other sectors and types of investments.
Some companies will be very expensive, a few will
reflect a fair value, and the majority will be offered
at a discount. Even though the underpriced REITs
are lesser-known corporations, you can still reap
substantial rewards by trading them.

They Don't Respond Well to Rising Interest Rates

Many investors think that REITs are highly sensitive to changes in interest rates. While they truly are sensitive, just like any other sector, changes in interest rates don't affect REITs more than they affect other investment instruments. If you observe historical charts, you'll find that in most periods and cases of rising interest rates, REITs performed better than the S&P 500. Interest rates are a reflection of the economy. When the economy is strong, there's likely a growing demand for real estate. Higher demand leads to increasing prices, rents, and occupancy rates. Even though the interest expense will grow, this won't offset the growing cash flow.

They Are Overleveraged

This strongly held belief mainly developed during the great financial crisis. At the time, there were very few lending requirements and banking standards and regulations. Nearly anyone who walked into a bank and applied for a loan walked out with approval. This, of course, resulted in an overleverage and a real estate market crash, making it difficult for REITs to refinance. As a result, they substantially cut their dividends and raised new capital, diluting the ownership of the existing investors.

In today's world, it's much harder to get a loan. Borrowers have to meet stronger credit scores and show their assets, history, and income before they get approved. REITs have also deleveraged their balance sheet, and interest coverage has significantly expanded, which means that they have stronger financial backing. Some professionals might even argue that REITs are underleveraged today.

REITs are perfect investment instruments for anyone who wishes to grow their wealth. Their versatility and the wide array of options available for investors make them an attractive choice for many, regardless of age, capital, and financial goals. REITs make a great addition to investment portfolios, offering a good opportunity to diversify.

Chapter 2:

Should You Invest in REITs?

With the endless investment opportunities available in the market, it can be hard to determine which ones are right for you. Fortunately, this chapter will help you decide whether REITs are suitable for your financial and investment goals. It will give you insight into what REITs in today's markets are like. You'll also understand the benefits of investing in them and the risks that you need to account for.

REITs in Today's Markets

The world is suffering from a dramatic increase in prices. In some parts of the world, the value of currencies fluctuates daily. Some people wake up to find that they have less money than they did before. Prices of wages, operating, and raw materials are also on the rise, severely affecting corporations and their stock prices. Inflation is inevitable in today's world.

REITs can serve as an inflation hedge for those who wish to grow or at least maintain the value of their money. These investment instruments have proven to outpace inflation and perform well in these devastating environments over time. The value of the property appreciates with the rising prices, benefiting the associated cash flows in the process. Apartments, houses, hotels, and other short-term leases can be easily adjusted. Landlords can increase rents to alleviate some of the inflationary pressures. Even real estate with long-term leases, such as offices and retail properties, can protect against inflation through built-in policies like inflation-caused increases.

REITs aren't perfectly synced with the movements that take place in the stock market, which means that they react better to volatility and turbulence. Even though they're considered more resilient than the stock market, they do offer similar returns in the long run. The opportunity to receive regular dividend payments and yields of at least 4% makes REITs a great investment for modern-day environments where it's difficult to obtain consistent capital gains.

It's worth noting that if you observe historical charts, you'll likely notice that REITs didn't grow consistently over the decades. The OPEC-related recession that occurred from 1972 to 1974 notably affected asset prices. Don't let this discourage you, however. All markets experience great rises and falls. Many REITs also have longer maturity periods and fixed-rate debt, which means that short-term growth in interest rates wouldn't largely affect the cost of capital.

Other Considerations

The coronavirus outbreak has undoubtedly affected numerous industries. One of the most substantial impacts was on commercial and office spaces. Commercial, retail, and office spaces were left empty during the global lockdown measures. To this day, remote and hybrid work environments have become the new norm. Besides health and safety concerns, managers are starting to appreciate the potential benefits that hybrid work systems have on employee morale, productivity, and efficiency. These rising trends might be the reason why the office industry will be forever reshaped.

Some companies are already implementing employee and square-foot shrinkage measures, while other businesses are continuously experimenting with ways to sustain cost-effective operations. The effects that these changes will have on REITs are yet to be observed.

On the other hand, the pandemic has caused shoppers to appreciate the fun, interactivity, and freedom of physical and storefront shopping. While there is reason to believe that the convenience and evolution of e-commerce will replace brick-and-mortar retail, this doesn't seem to be the case. Global lockdowns have emphasized the need for physical business locations, stimulating the retail property industry.

Understanding how REITs are performing in modern markets and learning about the possible risks, opportunities, and implications can give you a solid ground for further research and allow you to make responsible investing decisions.

Why You Should Invest in REITs

REITs offer a wide array of benefits that make them an ideal candidate for nearly any investment portfolio. Besides providing dependable returns, they also contribute to portfolio diversification and generate dividend income.

They Perform Competitively in the Long Run

While past performance is not always an indicator of future occurrences, historical charts offer some insight into what you can expect from a certain investment. REITs have repeatedly proven to outperform stocks, especially small-cap ones, during many instances and periods of time. The only time when small-cap stocks performed better than REITs was over the last year. That said, REITs have been outpacing the Russell 1000 Index, which comprises large-cap stocks, over the last 20, and even 30 years. REITs have also been outperforming bonds over the last 4 decades.

They Serve as an Attractive Stream of Income

Most REITs pay very competitive dividends, making them a solid stream of income and long-term returns. They generally pay higher dividend yields than stocks because REITs must comply with IRS regulations that state that 90% of these companies' taxable incomes must be distributed yearly among the shareholders. Most REITs even end up paying out more than the stated amount because their cash flows go beyond the net income. This is due to the large amounts of annually recorded depreciation. Many REITs also exhibit a steady increase in paid-out dividends, with some raising their dividends annually.

They're Liquid Investments

Real estate, as an industry, makes for a very illiquid investment opportunity. For instance, if you have a property that you wish to sell, it would be a lengthy process. You'd first have to list it on several websites or agencies, host open houses, wait for an offer that you're willing to accept, and if you're lucky, you'll seal the deal without an unexpected hitch. It would take you at least a couple of months before you can transform your asset into cash, which isn't ideal if you have a financial emergency. Not to mention the additional agency, listing, or closing fees that you'd have to pay.

REITs, however, combine the benefits of the real estate industry with the advantages of highly liquid instruments. If you ever need your money, you can easily sell your shares to anyone. You also wouldn't have to pay transaction fees because most brokers that offer REITs don't require commissions.

They're Highly Transparent

While private REITs have to meet very few standards and requirements, publicly traded REITs are characterized by their high transparency. Auditors, independent parties, directors, financial media, and analysts regularly monitor the performance of these investment trusts. All financial results are also revised by the SEC, making REITs a very safe instrument to invest in.

They Offer a Great Opportunity for Diversification

If you already have stock and bond investments, you should reduce your risk by investing in a different market, like real estate. This will allow you to mitigate your risk while possibly increasing your returns. REITs contribute to risk-adjusted returns that offset the volatility of the stock and bond markets.

The Risks of Investing in REITs

REITs are not considered highly risky investments, especially if they're carried as a part of a diversified portfolio. Some REITs comprise diversified holdings themselves, which is something that we will explore in more depth in Chapter 4. The main concerns of trading REITs are that they're subject to taxes and are generally sensitive to changes in interest rates. Like all investments, if you concentrate your capital on a single sector, you will experience great losses if the industry is negatively affected. You should also keep in mind that if you don't check whether the REITs you decide to invest in are registered, you might be defrauded and sell a scammy investment.

You should completely steer away from private REITs due to their low levels of transparency and nearly non-existent regulation. With that in mind, the following are some risks that you need to know before you decide to invest in non-traded and publicly traded REITs:

Risks of Investing in Non-Traded REITs

Since non-traded REITs are not available on the stock exchange, they come with several types of risks.

- **Difficult to Determine Share Value**

Since non-traded REITs are not available for public trading, you can't conduct thorough research on the performance of your investment. This makes it difficult to determine their value. Some public non-traded REITs eventually make these revelations 18 months after the deal is sealed.

- **High Illiquidity**

Unlike publicly-traded REITs, non-traded investments are characterized by their illiquidity. You won't always find someone willing to buy your REIT if you need to sell it, and oftentimes, your holding can't be sold for at least 7 years. While you might be able to obtain an amount of your investment in a year, you'll likely pay a fee.

- **Locked-In Investor Money**

Non-traded REITs need to collect as much money as possible to buy, maintain, operate, and manage real estate. This forces them to lock in the money of the investors and even pay out some of the dividends from this equity instead of using property-generated income. This limits cash flows and reduces the value of shares.

- **Additional Fees**

While this isn't really a risk, you should know that non-traded REITs charge between 9 to 10% and, in some cases, 15% of upfront fees. If well-managed, non-traded REITs can yield great returns. However, in that case, you'll likely have to pay management fees. Make sure to ask all questions and opt for as much transparency as you can before you invest in public non-traded REITs.

Risks of Investing in Publicly Traded REITs

While publicly traded REITs are a lot safer and more transparent than non-traded REITs, they still come with a few risks that you need to beware of.

- **Rising Interest Rates**

Historical data trends suggest that REITs perform better than stocks when interest rates rise. That said, REITs are also often negatively affected during periods of increasing interest rates. Higher interest rates cause a state of uncertainty among the public, which is why people invest their money in safer instruments, such as U.S. treasuries. Unlike REITs, stocks, corporate bonds, ETFs, and similar investments, treasures pay a fixed interest rate because the government guarantees them. It can be argued, however, that high interest rates reflect strong economies, which means the occupancy rates and rents are also rising.

- **Investing in the Wrong REIT**

You can lose a lot of money if you invest in the wrong REIT. Say you invest in one that has exposure to a suburban mall. You haven't done enough research, which is why you don't know that these types of shopping centers have suffered a sharp decline. The problem with REITs is that trends are always changing, so you always have to ensure that the holdings carried by the REIT in consideration are relevant to modern trends and will generate income.

- **Tax Implications**

One last thing you need to account for is that you'll have to pay taxes for your REIT dividends just as you would on your regular income. This is usually higher than what you'd pay for stock dividends or capital gains.

Now that you have read this chapter, you know everything you need to know before you invest in REITs. Understanding how REITs performed in the past, how they can help you today, and how they're relevant to the modern market can help you determine if this investment is right for you. Learning about the benefits and risks of investing in REITs can also help you assess whether it's suitable for your portfolio and financial goals.

Chapter 3:

Choosing REIT

Choosing the wrong REITs can cost you a lot of time, energy, and money. It's a risk that you don't want to take. In this chapter, you'll learn how to choose the right REITs to invest in based on their performance, your portfolio, and your financial and investment goals. You'll also understand how to assess and value REITs.

How to Choose the Right REITs

Here are some factors you should look into when searching for a REIT to invest in:

Explore Different Sectors

Some sectors have already reached their highest potential, such as residential and apartment REITs, which many investors had predicted the sudden rising interest in. Explore various sectors, observe current and upcoming trends, and conduct thorough research. Find REITs that have not yet fully recovered from the economic downturn, but make sure that the curve is pointing upward. Some interesting REITs you can explore are ones that are related to the distribution and warehouse industries.

Be Open to International Markets

Modern-day technology has diminished the geographic barriers that limit our ability to grow wealth and develop skills. Investors are no longer limited to national investment opportunities, especially when they can yield higher returns on international bonds and stocks. Similarly, you should open yourself up to international real estate markets and opportunities.

Don't Overlook the Net Asset Value

A REIT's net asset value is a key indicator of the per-share value of the investment trust. You can check if it's fairly, under-, or over-priced by taking a look at this number. You can also estimate the after-debt worth of the properties that the company carries.

Evaluate the Balance Sheets

The problem with trading and investing is that some opportunities can get popular very quickly, allowing investors to make hefty short-term profits. Many people allow their FOMO to take over and hop onto the bandwagon without checking the company's financial standing. Observe the company's profit margins and projections for several years, and check its debt-to-equity ratio. You can find credible information on the publicly traded companies database on the federal government's website. If you're going to make a sizable IPO investment, you can use specialized services to conduct thorough analyses and research on the company's fair value, practices, and operations.

Understand the Company

You should always put time and effort into understanding the company and its operations. Find out more about the internal controls of the business, the reliability of the management, where and how it generates most of its profits, the size of its market share, and the outlook and performance of the industry as a whole. Look into future performance projections for the business and the sector, as well. You don't want to invest in something that you don't fully understand.

Be Mindful of the Risks

While there are some general risks to investing in REITs, some risks are company and sector-specific. Make sure to understand all the problems you may encounter when dealing with the REITs you're considering investing in. If possible, speak to a representative and ask as many questions as you want beforehand.

Review the Dividend Yield and History

You need to review the current annual dividend yield of the REITs you're considering. More often than not, the dividends will be higher than what stocks offer because REITs have to distribute 90% of their income among shareholders. Many investors find it best to invest in REITs that yield around 5% to 6%, which might be lower than what other real estate investment opportunities often yield. What's even more important than the dividend yield is the REIT's dividend history. You want to make sure that the company has maintained a good historical streak of dividend payments. You want to invest in a REIT that proves to grow its dividends over time. This is a sign that it is performing well and gaining higher profits. Increasing dividends allow you to outpace inflation or at least maintain the value of your investment as all the prices go up. Good management practices suggest that the company has the shareholders' interest at heart.

Look into the Types of Property It Carries

If you have other real estate investments, investing in REITs is a great opportunity to gain exposure to sectors that you otherwise wouldn't have access to. This can further diversify your portfolio and open you up to a whole new world of rewards and opportunities. Let's say you're an engineer who rents a residential property for extra income on the side. Opting for REITs that carry healthcare properties, shopping malls, educational institutions, or other commercial and retail properties can be very beneficial. This type of investment also allows you to invest in specialized real estate, which means that you can reap the benefits of sectors that show potential future growth. Unless you have millions of dollars to spare, for instance, you can only invest in industries like tech and robotics through REITs.

How to Assess a REIT

Learning to assess REITs is vital when choosing the right interest trust to invest in. Investing in REITs has a lot in common with reading stocks on exchanges. While, for the most part, they're assessed like stocks, there are a few differences that you must take into consideration.

Factor in the Economy

The overall state of the economy substantially impacts the performance of the real estate industry and REITs. While you should note the general performance of the economy, you need to explore how the sector of interest is doing. For instance, if the company owns hospitality properties, you should look into the outlook of the hospitality sector. If you're investing in diversified REITs, take a close look at the portfolio and identify the overall outlooks of the industries involved.

Yield and Frequency

You might be tempted to invest in a REIT because it offers higher yields. Remember, however, that companies that offer really attractive yields might not necessarily provide stable and reliable dividend distributions. That said, lower yields aren't always indicators of stable income, nor are they always under-valued and safer investments.

Many beginners mistakenly take the history of yields as an indicator of the company's future performance. This isn't an accurate indicator, but it's always a useful measure of the company's ability to maintain consistent payouts. Choose a REIT that follows a distribution frequency schedule that aligns with your preferences. Investors who like regular payments opt for quarterly payouts rather than annual or semi-annual payouts.

Going Interest Rates

REITs are sensitive to changes in interest rates. If people expect interest rates to increase all of a sudden, REITs will become very volatile. While high-interest rates are likely to discourage people from buying real estate, they don't always lead to the underperformance of REITs. The returns of this asset class have historically proven to have a positive correlation with interest rates. While lower interest rates do encourage companies to refinance their loans before they mature and take new ones to expand their businesses, low-interest rates are indicators of weak economies. If a recession is to take place, REITs, along with other dividend classes, will suffer.

Weighted Average Lease Expiry

The weighted average lease expiry is the key to assessing how well a REIT is performing. This metric measures the average time that the leases of a REIT have before they expire. The expiry period depends on the area where the tenants reside and the rent they pay. A lower weighted average lease expiry is advantageous during periods of great economic growth. This means that the demand for real estate properties is higher than the supply, allowing managers to increase the prices of new rental contracts. On the other hand, longer weighted average lease expiries are reassuring to investors when the economy is rather weak. A longer WALE means that the tenants are constrained to contractual agreements for longer periods, providing stable rent.

Funds from Operations

While stock investors look at indicators like earnings per share and net income to determine how much money a company earns, these are not the best metrics to use when assessing REITs. Instead, you can use a measure known as funds from operations to effectively calculate the cash flow that a REIT's operations generate.

How to Value REIT

There is no handbook or guidelines to follow when assessing the value of any asset. No method is superior to the other, and chances are that each one will give you an entirely different answer and indicator. This is why you should know the basics of valuing stocks yourself, depending on your personal and portfolio needs.

Here are some metrics that you can use to estimate the value of REITs to decrease your risks and make sound investment decisions:

Debt-to-EBITDA

This ratio allows you to compare a REIT's leverage to that of others. Most companies disclose their debt-to-EBITDA ratio, so you won't need to calculate it yourself. While there isn't a standard debt to EBITDA to opt for, you should avoid companies that project much higher numbers than their competitors or other players in the industry.

Price-to-FFO

Funds from operations are usually publicly disclosed. You can use the price-to-FFO ratio to determine whether a REIT is expensive, cheap, or fairly priced relative to other companies in the industry.

Credit Rating

The credit ratings of a REIT can give you insight into the company's financial standing. Better debt ratings are also an indicator of how affordable it is for a company to borrow funds. Higher ratings are correlated with higher REIT values, so look for companies with investment-grade ratings.

Payout Ratio

You can figure out how sustainable a REIT's payouts are; you can look at its payout ratio. This metric portrays the dividends as a percentage of profit. When calculating this number, compare the dividend to the FFO rather than the net income. Average payout ratios are often 70% to 80%. While

100% and beyond can seem attractive, these numbers are often indicators of oncoming dividend cuts.

Adjusted FFO

Most companies disclose company-specific metrics, such as adjusted FFO. This number shows you the actual profitability of the REIT. If available, use this metric to calculate your price-to-FFO ratio for more accurate results.

Knowing how to choose the right REITs for your needs, portfolio, and goals will allow you to diminish your investment risks and increase your rewards. Investing in the wrong assets can prove to be incredibly costly, which is why it's always best if you assess, value, and compare all your options before you dive right in.

Chapter 4:

Diversifying with REITs

By reading this chapter, you'll learn what portfolio diversification is and why it's important. You'll also find a step-by-step guide explaining how to diversify your investment portfolio and lower your risks. Then, you'll learn how you can use REITs to diversify your portfolio and know which REIT sectors to invest in based on future projections. Finally, you'll understand what diversified REITs are and what they're good for and learn all about their risks.

What Is Diversification and Why Is It Important?

Diversification is an approach that encourages you to invest in various sectors and asset classes to limit your exposure to a specific type of asset. If one asset class or industry takes a dive, you would have other assets to neutralize or offset the risk of losing your money. When you don't put all your eggs in one basket, you decrease the volatility of your investment portfolio. The key to smart diversification practices is finding the right balance between your time horizon and risk tolerance. If you're too frugal with your investments, you won't be able to match the value of your investments to the rate of inflation. In other words, inflation will outpace the growth rates of your investments. Not following a specific timeline also increases your risk of not being able to meet your financial goals (ex: not having enough money to retire with). On the other hand, being an aggressive investor is more likely to cause you to put all your savings at risk of market volatility.

While diversifying your assets won't guarantee you don't lose any money, it will allow you to find the right balance between the amount of risk you're willing to accept and the level of rewards you expect to receive for those risks. The main aim of diversifying your investment portfolio shouldn't be to increase your returns but should be to lower your risks. A diversified portfolio mainly includes domestic stocks, bonds, international stocks, and short-term investments. For additional diversification, investors start including real estate funds, such as REITs, Sector funds, asset allocation funds, and commodity-focused funds.

How to Diversify Your Investment Portfolio

1. Asset Allocation

Riskier investments always yield higher returns, and the opposite is true. This is why asset allocation is the hardest aspect of portfolio diversification. You need to review your financial goals, the budget that you have to spare, and your risk tolerance. An investor who has some money to spare and is willing to put it at risk for the possibility of gaining higher rewards might invest 70% of their savings in stocks and the rest in bonds. Stocks are relatively riskier and offer higher rewards than bonds. An older investor who's on the verge of retirement would be more concerned with earning a stable income than increasing their wealth. In that case, they'd invest most of their savings in low-risk instruments like bonds and U.S. treasuries.

2. Understand the Risks

Always analyze and understand the risks before you take on any investment. Conduct the necessary research, observe the relative charts, evaluate performance history, check regulatory compliance, and value the asset before you make an investment decision. Make sure you're well-versed in the industry and the company's practices and operations.

3. Include Money Market Securities

Make room for money market securities in your portfolio, such as commercial papers, certificates of deposit, and treasury bills, because they're low-risk and highly liquid assets. They can come in handy during emergencies.

4. Include Systematic Cash Flow Bonds

This asset class allows you to withdraw certain amounts quarterly or even monthly. You're free to choose whether you wish to withdraw certain fixed amounts or ones that are based on your profits. This investment ensures stable cash flows and allows you to transfer fixed amounts of money between several mutual funds.

5. Study the Markets

You should know that you're committing yourself to a lifetime of studying and observing global and financial markets the moment you decide to become an investor. You need to understand all factors that influence movements in the market and how to act and take advantage of all cases. Keeping an eye on the market also gives you insight into which assets to invest in and which ones to sell.

6. Keep Your Investments Balanced

Building your investment portfolio is not a one-time endeavor. Besides the changes in the market, you'll be surprised to find that your financial goals and risk tolerance change over time. This is why you'd have to constantly fine-tune your portfolio to ensure that it matches your current needs.

7. Give Systematic Investment Plans a Try

It's okay if you don't have a large amount of money to invest all at once. You can try a systematic investment plan that allows you to allocate a small portion of your money toward mutual fund investments each month.

8. Make Room for Real Estate

Real estate investments are a great way to diversify your portfolio, increase your rewards, and reduce your risks. You don't need to save a lump sum to buy and rent a property to tenants, as you can invest in REITs instead.

Using REITs to Diversify Your Portfolio

Since REITs are not always positively correlated to stocks and bonds, it makes sense to add them to your portfolio. You should know that correlation between those asset classes does happen at times, however. Unfortunately, you'll never be able to foresee periods during which REITs offer similar returns to bonds or stocks or react to environmental changes the same way their either asset class would. This is why adding REITs to your portfolio shouldn't be a temporary venture or a means of reducing your investments' volatility for a period of time- you should hold them at all times.

Since mortgage REITs don't invest in the assets themselves and are often regarded as debt instruments, you should opt for equity REITs if your goal is portfolio diversification. If your portfolio is split between stocks and bonds, you should consider allocating at least 3% of your investments toward equity REITs.

The reason why REITs are less volatile than stocks is that they invest in hard assets. The value of REITs is directly determined by their correspondent real estate. Since the prices of properties don't fluctuate as quickly as stock prices, REITs are relatively more stable and consistent in value.

REIT Sectors That Can Contribute to a Diversified Portfolio

The following REIT sectors are worth eyeing if you wish to diversify your portfolio using REITs:

- **Industrial REITs**

With the rise of e-commerce and e-business operations, industrial REITs that comprise storage and fulfillment facilities and warehouses have never been more popular.

- **Data Center REITs**

While they can be costly to operate and maintain, data centers are becoming more popular as remote working opportunities and online shopping habits have become widely adopted.

- **Retail REITs**

People have learned to appreciate the importance of brick-and-mortar stores ever since the lockdown measures instigated by the coronavirus outbreak.

- **Residential REITs**

Multifamily properties that offer communities and home parks are on the rise.

- **Healthcare REITs**

The healthcare industry isn't negatively affected by periods of recession because it's a perpetual need for the public. Investing in this industry can alleviate some of your worries during economic downturns.

- **Infrastructure REITs**

While these REITs don't invest in traditional properties, they are associated with assets that are needed to operate a functional and connected society. Infrastructure REITs encompass cell phone towers, wireless infrastructure, energy pipelines, fiber cables, and more.

- **Self-Storage REITs**

Self-storage facilities have grown much more in demand since the coronavirus outbreak. People find it easier to have a place to store their belongings as they navigate the challenge of rising rent and home prices, and other lifestyle changes.

Diversified REITs

Diversified REITs often invest in several types of commercial real estate assets. Their portfolios often include a collection of several assets, including:

- Multifamily properties
- Healthcare institutions like hospitals and clinics
- Medical office buildings
- Resorts and hotels
- Warehouses
- Industrial facilities
- Retail properties, shops, malls, and other shopping buildings and centers
- Gas stations and similar infrastructure
- Travel centers
- Self-storage facilities
- Mixed-use properties

Most of these companies are involved with single-tenant net lease properties, as they're fortified with long-term protection by the triple-net leases. These types of contracts hold the tenant responsible for insurance, property taxes, and maintenance, which reduces the cost of owning real estate and allows the REIT to generate positive and consistent cash flows.

Other diversified REITs, however, especially ones that are tied to short-term leases and highly variable costs, usually experience income variability and a lack of consistency. REITs that invest in properties that require a third-party manager to oversee day-to-day operations are also known for yielding variable rental incomes.

It's worth noting that diversified REITs don't invest in random properties. They come up with a solid investment strategy surrounding a particular area of interest. For instance, one diversified REIT might be interested in certain types of properties, while another might diversify its real estate holdings within a particular city.

Diversified REITs quickly and easily expose you to a large spectrum of commercial real estate, allowing you to offset your risks. These companies make investing in real estate exponentially easier. Diversified REITs often pay out most of their cash flow through dividends, increasing their payout ratios. While this isn't necessarily a bad thing, it might increase the risk of dividend cuts, especially if some properties experience setbacks. This structure might also hinder the growth of the REIT, making it debt reliant. Other risks associated with diversified REITs depend on the types of properties they carry.

You should now have sufficient knowledge to build a diversified investment portfolio that allows you to actively manage your risks. Now that you've come across potentially rewarding REIT sectors to invest in and learned about the opportunities that diversified REITs provide, you are ready to come up with a successful investment strategy.

Chapter 5:

Getting Started with REITs

Having sufficient knowledge is not always enough to get you started. Theoretical information can be very confusing to turn into results if you don't know how to put it into practice. By reading this chapter, you'll understand how to make the best use of all the knowledge you gained about REITs so you can finally use them to generate profits and diversify your investment portfolios. You'll also learn about common mistakes that beginners make so you can avoid them.

Step-by-Step Guide: Investing in REITs

1. Remember How Different REITs Work

Touch up on the differences between mortgage, equity, and hybrid REITs to determine which of them aligns with your needs. While mortgage REITs are debt instruments, equity REITs are perfect for portfolio diversification. Many investors prefer hybrid

REITs because they combine the benefits of each. Depending on your risk tolerance, you should also decide whether you're interested in non-traded RE-ITs. Look at future projections and current performance indicators of various real estate sectors to identify the direction that you're headed in.

2. Consider the Risks

Don't overlook any of the risks of investing in REITs just because you're afraid you'll miss out on potential rewards. Making minor mistakes and overlooking small details can cost you a lot of time, money, and effort. Explore the risks that come with each type of REIT and real estate sector and weigh the benefits and rewards against the risks. Always estimate the risk-to-reward ratio of your investments and compare it to your risk tolerance, portfolio, and financial needs.

3. Set an Investment Budget

Observe your current investments and calculate their risk-to-reward ratio. Determine the percentage of your portfolio you need to allocate toward REITs to offset some of your risks. Once you have an estimate, you need to figure out how much money you are willing to invest in this asset class. While it's less volatile than its counterparts, it still carries some level of risk. If you wish to invest in different REITs, assess the different risk levels that they carry and allocate a portion of your budget toward each accordingly. Be mindful of the level of liquidity of the REITs in consideration, as this would also affect how you choose to distribute your budget.

4. Choose Your REIT(s)

Once you've come up with candidates to choose from, learn about their operations and industries. Check each of the REIT's management track records, find indicators and charts of past and current performance, and compare them to other players in the industry. Find out as much information as you can about the companies in consideration. Learn more about the incentives and compensation plans offered to the managers and dig up any additional investment fees. This will either bring your attention to potential red flags or give you the green light to go ahead and invest. Check the earnings of the company and pay attention to metrics like debt-to-EBITDA, debt-to-FFO, credit rating, payout ratio, and adjusted FFO.

If you're planning to invest in diversified REITs, check out the companies that they invest in. You shouldn't be alarmed if you find that the REIT is heavily concentrated on a specific type of real estate property. However, if market conditions and environmental changes seem to affect that industry heavily, you should consider investing in a different REIT.

5. Set Up Your Brokerage Account

Once you're positive about your choice, set up your brokerage account to get started. If you already have other investments, using the same brokerage account for your REITs venture makes sense. If you're new to the trading world, compare different brokerage options to find a platform that you feel comfortable dealing with. Opt for brokerages that don't request commissions on trades, offer helpful features like charts, tools, and resource libraries, and have a user-friendly platform. Once you sign up on a platform, you'll likely be asked to make your initial deposit. You can start trading as soon as the money is transferred to your account.

Common Mistakes to Avoid

REITs have maintained their status as high-returning asset classes over the past two decades. Averaging a whopping annual 13% ROI, REITs have drawn the attention of numerous investors. Many people invest in REITs thinking that they, too, will immediately make 13% of returns every year. However, this isn't always the case. Many new investors fail to meet their expected returns because they continue making few yet costly common errors. Here are a few mistakes that beginner REIT investors make and how you can avoid them:

Selling Low

"Buy low, sell high" is the first and most well-known rule of trading. When the REIT market suffers major losses, you need to take a step back and ask yourself if you want to opt-out just because the REIT has decreased in value or because you think that it will further. Keep in mind that the expectations of the investors often dictate the actual movement of a REIT. Traders build their expectations based on their interpretations of various data, including economic status, market conditions, occupancy rates, and so on. Even though prices are always changing, new information needs to stimulate the shift in expectations first. In other words, you need to take it to social media and news outlets to gain insights into the expectations of the public before you make any rash decisions. If the good news is circulating, people will become more optimistic, and the REIT will move in a more positive direction. You'll regret selling near the bottom of the REIT picks up again.

Sticking to the Trader Mindset

If you're not new to investing and trading, you might feel inclined to think like a trader. While it might take some time, real estate properties eventually increase in value and yield some revenue. Many people struggle to apply this concept to REITs because they're relatively much more liquid than flat-out buying a house. It's not easy to turn a solid property into cash. However, if you invest in a publicly-traded REIT, you can easily sell it to someone else. This is why many investors constantly trade in and out of positions, especially those who can't lose the trader mentality. They are obsessed with observing daily market charts and fluctuations, forgetting that REITs are long-term investments tied to hard real estate assets. Frequent trades leave you with accumulating tax payments and deny you the opportunity to receive consistent dividends.

Allowing Fear to Take Over

Many investors are reluctant to increase their share even after analyzing the company and the sector and ensuring that future projections look good. If you're certain that the current price of the REIT is considered a discount compared to what you'll earn in the future, you should buy more. Similarly, you shouldn't be quick to buy a REIT just because you're worried you'll miss out on what you think is a great bargain. Not all discounted assets are stolen opportunities because a declining price is associated with negative expectations. It could also be an indicator of an oncoming dividend cut.

Not Growing

Many investors treat REITs as a one-time investment. Downturns present excellent opportunities to purchase REITs that were once out of your budget. Not only will you be adding high-performing assets to your portfolio, but you'd be decreasing its volatility in the process. Investing in a single REIT is okay until you get grips on the market and feel more comfortable with the idea. Once you've gained enough experience, don't be afraid to branch out and diversify your REIT portfolio.

Falling into Yield Traps

The excitement of earning reliable income compels investors to invest in high-yield investments without conducting thorough research. Most of these REITs aren't able to sustain these payouts in the long term. While this doesn't apply to all high-yielding REITs, many companies overleverage their interest trusts and have high payout ratios just to attract more investors. Not only does this trigger a dividend cut, but it also substantially decreases the value of the REIT. Opt for high-quality companies that can sustain long-term dividend payouts- those usually have a 5% to 8% yield. High-yielding trusts managed by external managers and REITs offering more shares and diluting their shareholder equity are also red flags.

Selling Too Quickly

You might be tempted to sell your REIT quickly if offered an attractive price. It's an opportunity to secure good gains, after all. If you ever feel compelled to sell right away, take a step back and consider all the potential rewards you can miss out on if you sell too soon. Observe the charts and learn more about the public's expectations before making a decision. Many sell at an attractive price only to watch their REITs skyrocket. Nothing is more tempting than quick and instant profits, but make sure that you won't regret it later.

Just like opting out just because the price of the REIT has fallen can be a horrible mistake, selling as soon as it increases in value isn't smart either. REITs that increase in price aren't necessarily overvalued.

Now that you read this chapter, you know how to put all your knowledge into practice so you can finally generate passive income from investing in REITs. You also understand which mistakes to watch out for and how to avoid making them.

Conclusion

In the 1960s, the federal government made a decision that would forever add new dimensions and possibilities to real estate investments. Everyone- not just banks and millionaires- is now able to invest in sizable properties and commercial real estate. The benefits that come with this opportunity, however, have only been fully embraced and recognized during the last decade.

More investors are starting to consider trading REITs because of the low-interest rate environment. Instead of limiting themselves to bonds and similar investment instruments, people with a growth mindset are now searching for new ways to generate income. The surfacing of real estate-focused mutual funds and ETFs has stimulated a newly-found hunger among investors- many people now wish to invest in real estate. Since not everyone has millions of dollars to spare on specialized and large-scale properties, REITs sound like a very appealing investment opportunity.

More and more investors who once overlooked this asset class are now starting to appreciate all the benefits that REITs have to offer. These interest trusts offer relatively high dividends and yields, have low transaction costs and aren't largely correlated to the stock market, making them a great portfolio diversification tool. REITs can be used to offset or at least neutralize the risks imposed by other investments, especially during periods of stock market volatility and turbulence. Investing in the right REITs can also allow you to outpace inflation or at least preserve the value of your money during these rough periods.

There are several risks, however, that you need to account for if you wish to invest in REITs. While publicly traded trusts are the safest type of REITs to invest in, given their high transparency and close regulation, choosing the wrong one can cost you a lot of money. You should be careful while trading non-traded REITs and avoid private REITs at all costs. The latter are highly illiquid, and the companies are characterized by their low transparency.

You need to consider many risks when choosing the right REIT for your financial and investment goals. Make sure to conduct a rounded and thorough assessment of your options instead of basing your decision on a specific metric, such as high yields. For example, undervalued REITs can be very attractive. However, they might also be overleveraged. Don't make any rash decisions, and take your time to understand the company and its industry. Compare the results of your assessments, research, and valuation to your portfolio's needs and risk tolerance.

Now that you have read this book, you are ready to safely and successfully start building passive income from real estate investment trusts.

References

7 REIT sectors that can help you diversify your portfolio. (n.d.). The Motley Fool. https://www.fool.com/slideshow/7-reit-sectors-that-can-help-you-diversify-your-portfolio/?slide=8

Ashworth, W. (2010, June 3). 5 types of REITs and how to invest in them. Investopedia. https://www.investopedia.com/articles/mortgages-real-estate/10/real-estate-investment-trust-reit.asp

Askola, J. (2020, March 17). Top reasons to not invest in REITs. Seeking Alpha. https://seekingalpha.com/article/4331270-top-reasons-to-not-invest-in-reits

Askola, J. (2021, July 18). The 5 most common REIT investing errors. Seeking Alpha. https://seekingalpha.com/article/4439636-the-5-most-common-reit-investing-errors

Chen, J. (2003, November 25). Real estate investment trust (REIT): How they work and how to invest. Investopedia. https://www.investopedia.com/terms/r/reit.asp

Choosing the right REIT. (n.d.). RegionsBank. https://www.regions.com/insights/wealth/taxes-and-estate-planning/planning-tax-strategies/choosing-the-right-reit

DiLallo, M. (n.d.-a). Are REITs a good investment? The Motley Fool. https://www.fool.com/investing/stock-market/market-sectors/real-estate-investing/reit/are-reits-a-good-investment/

DiLallo, M. (n.d.-b). Investing in diversified REITs. The Motley Fool. https://www.fool.com/investing/stock-market/market-sectors/real-estate-investing/reit/diversified-reit/

Esajian, P. (2022, June 3). 10-step guide to diversifying your portfolio. FortuneBuilders. https://www.fortunebuilders.com/diversify-your-real-estate-investment-portfolio-2/

How I select the best real estate investment trusts (REITs). (2021, May 13). Marcoschwartz.com.

https://marcoschwartz.com/how-i-select-the-best-real-estate-investment-trusts-reits

How to evaluate and analyze REITs. (n.d.). DBS. https://www.dbs.com.sg/personal/articles/nav/investing/evaluating-reits

James Royal. (2022, September 26). 5 REIT investing mistakes to avoid. Bankrate; Bankrate.com. https://www.bankrate.com/investing/reit-investing-mistakes-to-avoid/

Luthi, B. (2022, February 17). Step-by-step guide on how to invest in REITs. Experian.com; Experian. https://www.experian.com/blogs/ask-experian/how-to-invest-in-reits/

Matthew Frankel, C. F. P. (n.d.). How to value a REIT. The Motley Fool. https://www.fool.com/investing/stock-market/market-sectors/real-estate-investing/reit/how-to-value-reit/

Moskowitz, D. (2015, March 19). What are the risks of real estate investment trusts (REITs)? Investopedia. https://www.investopedia.com/articles/investing/031915/what-are-risks-reits.asp

Owning an equity REIT vs. A mortgage REIT: What's the difference? (2015, January 20). Investopedia. https://www.investopedia.com/ask/answers/012015/what-are-pros-and-cons-owning-equity-reit-versus-mortgage-reit.asp

Risk factors of investing in REITs. (2020, February 27). Corporate Finance Institute. https://corporatefinanceinstitute.com/resources/wealth-management/risk-factors-of-investing-in-reits/

Stalter, K. (2015, November 15). Use REITs to add portfolio diversification. Forbes. https://www.forbes.com/sites/katestalter/2015/11/15/use-reits-to-add-portfolio-diversification/?sh=64bb58a1151a

Voigt, K. (2017, October 2). Best-performing REITS: How to invest in real estate investment trusts. NerdWallet. https://www.nerdwallet.com/article/investing/reit-investing

What is portfolio diversification? - fidelity. (n.d.). Fidelity.com. https://www.fidelity.com/learning-center/investment-products/mutual-funds/diversification

What's a REIT (real estate investment trust)? (n.d.). Reit.com. https://www.reit.com/what-reit

Why invest? Motives for buying public offices. (2017). In The State as Investment Market (pp. 70–93). University of Pittsburgh Press.

Why REITs? And why now? (n.d.). Morgan Stanley Investment Management. https://www.morganstanley.com/im/en-us/individual-investor/insights/articles/why-reits-and-why-now.html

(N.d.). Etoro.com. https://www.etoro.com/news-and-analysis/investing/consider-reits-for-your-portfolio/